A gift for:

T0124070

From:

OTHER HELEN EXLEY GIFTBOOKS:

For my Mother 365	Friendship 365	Happy Days! 365
Senior Moments 365	Inspiration 365	Giggles 365
For my Sister 365	Calm Days 365	Yes to life! 365

Published in 2012 and 2021 by Helen Exley® LONDON in Great Britain.

Edited by Dalton Exley

Photography copyright © Yoneo Morita 2012, 2021 Hanadeka™
Licensed through Intercontinental Licensing
Words by Pam Brown © Helen Exley Creative Ltd 2012, 2021
Design, selection and arrangement © Helen Exley Creative Ltd 2012, 2021

ISBN 978-1-84634-669-9

12 11 10 9 8 7 6 5 4 3 2 1

The moral right of the author has been asserted. A copy of the CIP data is available from the British Library on request. All rights reserved. No part of this publication may be reproduced or transmitted in any form or by any means, electronic or mechanical, including photocopy, recording or any information storage and retrieval system without permission in writing from the Publisher. Printed in China.

Helen Exley® LONDON
16 Chalk Hill, Watford, Herts WD19 4BG, UK
www.helenexley.com

MIX
Paper from
responsible sources
FSC® C081635

JANUARY 1

There is nothing so beautiful as a sleeping cat.

WHAT IS A HELEN EXLEY GIFTBOOK?

Helen Exley has been creating giftbooks for twenty-seven years,
and her readers have bought more than 90 million copies of her
works in thirty-seven languages.

Because her books are bought as gifts, she spares no expense
in making sure that each book is as thoughtful and meaningful a gift
as it is possible to create: good to give, good to receive.

Team members help to find thoughtful quotations from literally hundreds
of sources, and the books are then personally created.

With infinite care, Helen ensures that each spread is individually
designed to enhance the feeling of the words and that the whole book
has real depth and meaning.

You have the result in your hands. If you have found it valuable –
tell others! We'd rather put the money into more good books
than waste it on advertising, when there is no power on earth
like the word-of-mouth recommendation of friends.

Dear cats. Dear best of friends.

A marvellous pose.
Turn. Reach for the
camera. Turn back.
He's gone.

There is always
a little lost cat
waiting to fill the gap
in your life.

DECEMBER 30

Cats are the superior species. But have enough sense to keep quiet about it.

So small – so full
of love and ingenuity.
So frail – so full of life.

DECEMBER 29

Cats never completely leave you. They side-step Time, shrug off Death – come at the call of memory. Their beauty undiminished. Their touch as gentle. Their love perpetual.

Every tiny
bundle of fur
is fully armed.

Cats have made
a profession
of being adorable.
It pays.

A dog looks guilty
if he's sinned.
A cat, never.

Cats lend us magic and the stuff of dreams.

Tread softly. The cat's asleep.

DECEMBER 26

Christmas is a time
for cats – trees to climb,
baubles to dab,
soft toys to throttle,
cream to lick, turkey
to steal. Boxes. Paper.
Ribbon. String.
And cuddles.

A little cat
has taught many a child
to care, to love.

A cat is a small
wild animal
that has chosen
comfort.

A cat brings beauty into
the dullest day.

Every tamed cat a small, amiable tyrant.

All cats – from
Bengal Tigers to alley cats
– are variations on a single
splendid theme.

A dog serves.
A cat is served.
Preferably with
haddock.

A little cat brings the jungle
into suburbia.

"Tricks?
I do tricks.
My own – and
when I choose"
says Cat

A cat purring soothes the most troubled heart.

DECEMBER 21

At any moment
of time someone
on earth is apologising
to a cat.

Best ask his owner
if you can pat his dog.
With cat, ask the cat.

A cat is loyal. But not very.

DECEMBER 20

A sleeping cat has discovered the secret of perfect content.

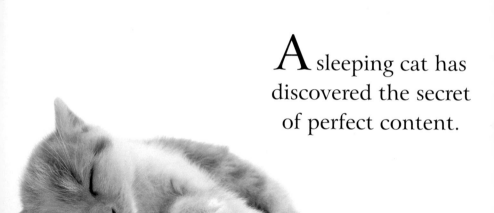

Every cat a feral
under the skin.

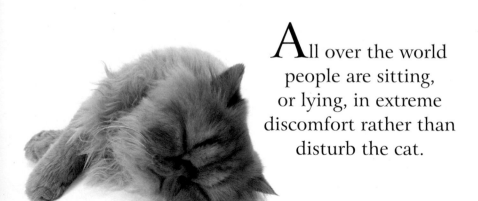

All over the world
people are sitting,
or lying, in extreme
discomfort rather than
disturb the cat.

A cat obeys rules. His.

DECEMBER 18

All cats have a surprise up their sleeves.

One owns a dog.
One co-operates
with a cat.

Even the most affectionate needs time to himself. "Of course I love you. Go away."

JANUARY 17

Cat long since achieved
Perfection
– and sees no reason
for further adjustment.

A cat loves cat toys just so long as you are prepared to put in the work.

A cat is an enigma.

Watch where you are treading.
I sleep where I want to sleep.

People are usually
honoured
when a cat decides
to like them.

DECEMBER 14

Be wary of cute kittens. They have something planned.

A dog who has broken something is full of regret and apology. A cat swears he was never near the thing.

Anyone who has a cat
suspects that it is psychic.

JANUARY 21

Try to learn Cat. It is a subtle language but well worth the effort.

DECEMBER 12

A kitten is only a beginning
– a prelude to the glory of
cathood.

A dog secretly hopes
that one day he will
become human.
A cat would be appalled
by the possibility.

DECEMBER 11

Any competent
psychiatrist confronted
with analysis of a feline
mind would be driven
to retirement
after a single session.

Even the most sedate
mog sometimes indulges
in a silly half hour.

A cat can always
manage a second breakfast
– donated by the kind
lady up the road.
Or a third.
Or a fourth.

Owner? Mistress?
Master?
Nothing applies.
Slave comes near it.

Cats know all
about cameras.
And which is their
Best Side.

A cat has mastered conservation of energy. If nothing demands his immediate attention – he simply switches off.

Cats never perform to order.

A cat will accept you
as companion and provider.
But not as his superior.

Anything Anti-cat
doesn't work.

Those who love cats
tickle, stroke, rub
and snuggle on request.
But warily.

DECEMBER 6

At last a cat food he's prepared to eat. Buy a crate. He'll never touch it again.

A cat loves you
after his fashion.
He does not
worship you.

DECEMBER 5

Feed me, stroke me,
scratch me
says the cat.
Arrange amusements.

When someone,
through age or loneliness
or grief finds love has left them,
they can often rediscover it
in a little cat.

Cats are not
Almost Human.
They are totally Cat.

JANUARY 30

Search a room
from top to bottom
for your missing cat.
Pause.
And your cat will
stroll out of it
with a supercilious
smile on his face.

DECEMBER 3

Cats are elasticated.

Cats know instinctively
who is good at tickling.

We learned
Lateral Thinking
from cats.

Ask any cat.
One does not need
opposable thumbs.

To laugh at a cat
who has missed
his footing is to
mortally offend him.

DECEMBER 1

Be alert. Your
cat can out-think
you.

The love of
a little cat
should never be
despised.

NOVEMBER 30

One is never bored
if one has a cat about
the house.
He sees to that.

A cat knows very well
what Go, Come, Stay mean.
He simply refuses
to acknowledge them
as applying to himself.
A cat gives instructions.
He does not take them.

Cats never lose the chance to steal a scene.

A cat is full of
Opinions.
But he keeps them
to himself.

Every cat – tiger
to tabby kitten –
is a masterpiece.

The human heart
clings to a fragile hope
that we will find each other
in eternity.

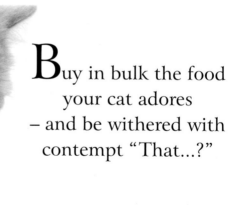

Buy in bulk the food
your cat adores
– and be withered with
contempt "That...?"

FEBRUARY 6

Warn a visitor that
your cat can be downright
dangerous if he
is picked up, turn away,
and subsequently find him
curled in her arms
eyes blissfully closed,
and purring fit to bust.

A bored cat is an inventive cat.

Scold a dog
and he cowers.
Scold a cat
and he washes
his paws.

NOVEMBER 25

Half way between
kitten and cat
is katten.
A creature of delight.

A cat refuses
to be bored.
He will either
invent a game
or sleep.

A cat is mystified
when you don't
understand his perfectly
clear conversation.

A cat hates above
any other thing
making a fool of itself.

NOVEMBER 23

Even a little cat
can prove that love
outlasts death.

FEBRUARY 10

A cat does not need
to demonstrate
his affection wildly.
A leaning against
your legs. A chirrup.
A gentle paw.
"I'm glad you're home."

NOVEMBER 22

Human beings, with patience and
tenacity, can be made to understand
a cat's demands. Food. Shelter.
Comfort. Those who are kind in
disposition learn. Those who are
not should be abandoned.
One can always find
another home.

With dogs you know exactly where you stand.. With a cat. Never.

A human being is to a cat
a scaled-up version
of its mother.
It cuddles close and accepts
her stroking in lieu of its
mother's tongue.
A kitten still.

There is enough of the wild
left in both cats and dogs
to justify a little caution.

Fire, flood or
earthquake.
What one treasure
would I choose to save?
You, of course,
dear cat.

No cat ever has a
Bad Hair Day.

"Get up"
says Cat.
"Spring has come.
Don't let's waste
a minute."

FEBRUARY 14

The oldest,
ugliest,
smelliest cat
can often be
the most loving.

NOVEMBER 18

"Fetch, Rover, fetch!"
Cat looks on:
"If you want the ball
you fetch it."

A cat adjusts
his demands
according to
the gullibility
of its human.

Every cat should
have a small jungle
to explore.
Even if it is merely
a cabbage patch.

People of importance
often turn to cats.
They neither flatter
nor fawn.

NOVEMBER 16

Dear cats that I have known I miss you still, remembering your eccentricities, your eyes golden or green, your conversation. You are the best of all the treasures I have gathered. I'll hold you safe forever.

People who need
to be worshipped
should not
choose a cat.

...his purr
overflows
his heart
to fill
the room.

A cat who doesn't
want to be found isn't.

NOVEMBER 14

Resign yourself.
You can have a cat
or furniture.

FEBRUARY 19

Even the most
sober-minded cat
cannot resist
a moving blob
of light.

NOVEMBER 13

I know my cat
loves me
– or I think he does.

When your cat
has the hump,
steer clear.

NOVEMBER 12

Every gesture
a cat makes is a
small perfection.

A cat understands
most of what you say
– but he finds it
judicious to pretend
that he doesn't.

Dogs need to know their place in The Pack. Cats haven't the faintest idea what a Pack is.

A cat is perfectly willing to fit in to your ways – providing he can retain his own.

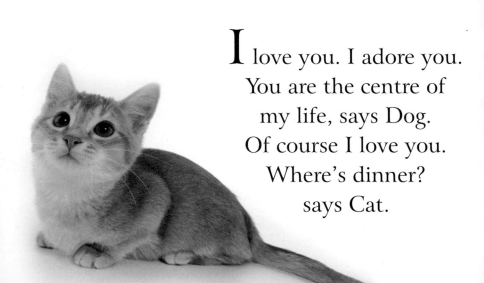

I love you. I adore you. You are the centre of my life, says Dog. Of course I love you. Where's dinner? says Cat.

FEBRUARY 23

The most devoted
cat owner
lives uneasily
with the suspicion
that his cat knows
more than he cares
to admit.

Every cat owner has the temptation to tie a little purse around their pussy's neck and send it down to the supermarket to choose what it's prepared to eat this week.

A cat keeps its secrets safe.

Every cat is convinced
he knows best.

One resents being
under another's
thumb but one
accepts being under
a paw.

All cats are beautiful
– even the ugly ones.

FEBRUARY 26

"Heel!" says
the dog owner.
And, with luck,
is obeyed.
"Don't be ridiculous,"
says cat.

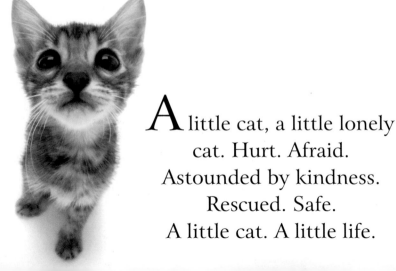

A little cat, a little lonely
cat. Hurt. Afraid.
Astounded by kindness.
Rescued. Safe.
A little cat. A little life.

FEBRUARY 27

A cat needs no words
– the touch of a little paw
– a whiskery kiss
– a drowsy purr
are enough to tell you
that he loves you.

NOVEMBER 5

A cat has
a wild and secretive
face, and the face
it shows
the one it loves.

FEBRUARY 28/29

Time passes. Things change. Says cat,
I let the current take me where it will
– and so remain content.

NOVEMBER 4

Every cat needs
to be comfortable
– at any cost.
It's wonderful how
far a small cat
can spread.

Owners say
their dogs are almost
human.
A cat would be
appalled.

Every cat is
a unique individual.
As are we all.

A cat does
what he planned to do.

Every cat knows that the solution to almost everything is sleep.

MARCH 3

A cat is a small
perfection
And knows it.

NOVEMBER 1

"Come" says Cat.
"Let's have a scamper."

A cat very quietly
reorganises your existence.

Every cat has
a secret life.

No cat is wholly domesticated.
Some fraction of his being will always be wild.
And this is why we cherish him.

OCTOBER 30

...a small cat
in the window,
a small cat at the door.
And there is love.

A cat that is looking
especially angelic
is up to something.

The smallest kitten
only needs a week
to be in full possession
of a house and
its owners.

A cat rearranges
your life
to suit his own.

Every cat
a tiger in disguise.

A cat has preferences.
He will let you know.

Every cat a critic.

One never quite gets
over the loss of cat.

Like flowers,
inexhaustible in beauty.
Like flowers, most
necessary – in ways
we scarcely understand.
Healers. Companions.
Mysteries.

Play a game
with your cat.
To his rules.

Dog whisperers.
Horse whisperers.
But no cat whisperers.

Go away, says cat.
I am concentrating.
I aim to achieve
the ultimate in sleep.

Every artist and writer needs a cat companion, critic, inspiration.

One never takes
a cat for a walk.
He may, of course,
choose to
accompany you.

Dogs are loyal.
Cats are loyal as long
as it suits them.

Shut the Christmas
turkey in the downstairs
loo for safety.
Two hours
later open the door
to release a happy cat
and a legless bird.

Dogs persuade us
we are gods.
Cats assure us
that we are not.

A cat never admits defeat. He just pretends he wasn't really interested in the first place.

Dogs wait patiently
or otherwise for
their masters.
Cats are long gone.

MARCH 15

A cat never
examines his
conscience.
He has none.

OCTOBER 20

Dogs, bless their hearts, are gullible. A cat believes absolutely nothing without proof.

A cat
has his reasons
which he's not
going
to explain.

Dog owners prefer
certain breeds.
Cat lovers like cats.

A dog dances with delight at the sight of its master, barks, leaps, scampers, rolls over, nuzzles, drools. A cat gives a restrained hello.

Every cat needs
a window on the world.

MARCH 18

A cat puts aside
yesterday
and does not plan
for his tomorrow.
He very wisely
lives simply for today.

The pleasure of living with a cat is that you never discover all its secrets.

A cat
who stares at you
for any length of time
is plotting something.
Prepare.

Dear cat.
You don't do much.
You mostly sleep and eat
and saunter round the
garden. And yet you seem
to need my company
as I do yours.

Over the centuries we have changed
   – in habits, clothing and belief
      – but cat is constant.
   Riding the pharaoh's punt
   through tall papyrus stems.
   Sprawled across a papal knee.
Sleeping beside an open kitchen fire.
   Bright-eyed in candlelight.
   They reach soft paws to us across
the years. Our dear familiar friends.

A cat will show
its outer beauty
to the world and
perhaps hint at its
affectionate heart.
All else is hidden kept
for the one it loves.

MARCH 21

A cat needs no tricks
to demand attention.
He is simply There.

After combing one's cat
he seems no thinner
yet one has acquired
enough fur
to build another cat.

Try dominating a cat, and he'll leave home.

It's a hard
heart a kitten
cannot melt.

No cat belongs
completely to any
human being –
a companion
but never
a possession.

OCTOBER 12

Every cat is
a scrounger at heart.

MARCH 24

We moved.
People phone.
Always to ask after
the cat.

Dear human, you believe you know what I am thinking – but you never do.

A cat outlives a flower,
a mouse, a summer.
But never long enough.
The heart
still yearns for him
long after he has gone.

Joy is to see
a little lost cat
ambling up
the garden path.

The laws
of physics do not
apply to cats.

Dear cat.
I can't switch
off the rain.
Forgive me.

Those who require obedience
should not acquire a cat.

Dog and Horse were
seen as Useful
and so were disciplined
to fit Man's needs.
Cat took no notice
and remains
simply and everlastingly
Himself.

Tickle my tummy.
Stroke my lovely fur.
Delight in my waving paws,
my reverberating song.
And I will clamp you.
And bite you to the bone.

People, in exasperation,
sometimes wonder whether
they own their cats,
or their cats own them.
The cats do not need
to spectulate.

A cat has a rich vocabulary
but we are too ignorant to
understand.

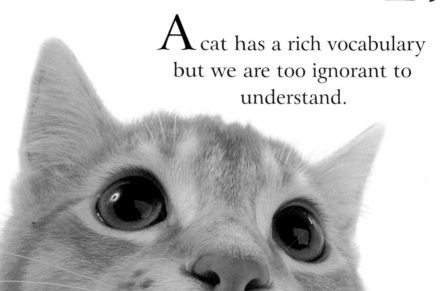

OCTOBER 6

Dear Missis,
I will love you with
at least half my heart.
The rest is reserved
for the lady next door,
who gives me smoked
salmon.

A bored cat is a restless cat
– looking for trouble.

OCTOBER 5

One has a quite exceptionally clever cat – and one tells one's friends. They come to call – and are confronted by an animal who appears to be not entirely right in the head. It stares at them blankly. "Me? I'm just a poor stupid pussy-cat." and goes away to laugh in some quiet corner.

A cat knows what
he knows but is not going
to let you know it.

A cat will vividly enact the chase with a dry leaf as a mouse – until some silly human being says, "Kill it. Kill the mouse!" When he will stare in disdain, "Mouse? For heaven's sake, can't you see it's a dead leaf!"

APRIL 1

Every cat, pampered
or scruffy,
stray or sheltered,
is utterly unique
and worthy of respect.

OCTOBER 3

A kitten can
and will fall off
almost anything.
But will never admit
it was an accident.

APRIL 2

Tinned fish. No.
Fresh Salmon, yes.

OCTOBER 2

A happy cat is a reverberating cat.

Call a dog
and he comes.
Call a cat
and he may.
Eventually.

There are cats who hide
in cupboards to avoid
visitors. And cats who
are downright embarrassing
in their efforts to win
their hearts.

There is nothing
so laid back
as a laid back cat.

Cats refuse to accept the word Domesticated.

A cat can beg,
implore, beseech
without twitching
a whisker.

A sulking cat
is solid sulk.

APRIL 6

A cat has
an infinite ability
to make one feel
guilty.

Curious how a newly
purchased rug grows
steadily more tufty
and bald in patches
almost overnight.
Cat knows the secret.

We can rarely guess what a cat is thinking. Maybe it's as well.

SEPTEMBER 27

Cats love a game
– but expect you to do
all the work.

Cat lovers
bear the scars.

A CAT
EXPECTS
TO BE
ADORED.

APRIL 9

A cat lover finds
friends
the world over.

The world is full
of dog lovers.
And cat obsessives.

A cat is wiser than
he wants you to recognise.

A cat does not speculate about its future. It does not analyze its past. It has no ambitions or regrets. It accepts the moment and makes the best of it.

A dog gobbles.
A cat picks,
savours
and delivers
judgement.

Cats have days
of melancholy
– and cannot tell
you why.

A cat is never lost
for something to do.
He can always sleep.

Centuries of practice
have made all cats
escapologists.

What is a cat?
Anything
that he decides to be.

A cat's gaze has
a quietness
that calms the
human heart.

A cat doesn't bark
or wag or scrabble
when he wants out.
He simply sits
and stares at you.

Cat says:
Now is the time
for stillness. Gentle my
fur and I will sing
for you. And my song
will soothe your heart
to quietness.

APRIL 15

A cat agrees to
live with you
– on his terms.

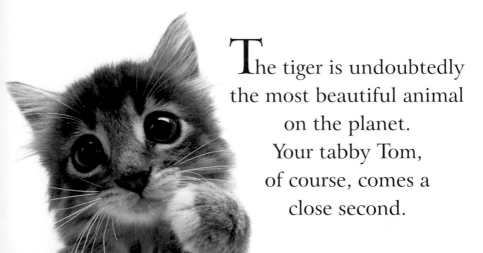

SEPTEMBER 19

The tiger is undoubtedly the most beautiful animal on the planet. Your tabby Tom, of course, comes a close second.

APRIL 16

You're never done
with a cat.
He sees to that.

SEPTEMBER 18

The words
No, Get Down,
Stop,
Leave it
mean nothing
to a cat.

"Who's a lovely boy, then?" And the dog rolls over in delight. The cat gives a withering look and leaves.

Live by his rules
and you and the cat
will get along
very well.

There is no such thing
as a cat owner.

SEPTEMBER 16

Anywhere
in the world you
can find someone to
Talk Cat with.

No cat is the same
as any other.

Dogs on the whole
are honest,
even showing guilt.
Cats lie habitually.

No cat cares
to explain
what he wants.
He lets you
work it out.

Round, misty-blue eyes stare desperately. Love me, they say, let me into your life – so that I can begin to take over your entire existence.

A hungry cat
is an insistent cat.

A great many cats
have, unknown to their
official owners,
several names –
given by neighbours
who have been hoodwinked
into believing they
are sad little strays.

APRIL 22

A cat sprawled
on its back
is waiting hopefully
for someone to pause
and rub his tum.

SEPTEMBER 12

Cats don't see why
they should waste time
learning words.
After all – they have
no intention
of obeying anyone.

We mourn the loss
of our cats. For they were
our companions.
Part of our lives.
Bound to us by love.
A little of the heartbreak
will stay with us forever.
A little of the joy
we knew together.

A cat is always on the wrong side of any door.

Every movement a cat
makes has been perfected
through millennia.
And he knows it.

SEPTEMBER 10

Turn away if your cat jumps short and hide your smile. No animal can be so deeply offended as a cat.

Nine out of ten cats adore this food they say. Me, I'm the one that doesn't.

Come to your call?
says cat.
Don't be ridiculous.
I have my self respect.

A cat cannot speak – but he can still give orders.

We seek beauty, poise, grace, elegance. The cat does not. He has them already.

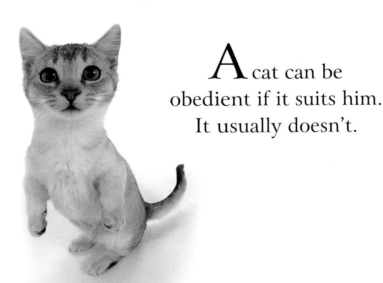

A cat can be
obedient if it suits him.
It usually doesn't.

One never ceases to find new wonders in a cat. Pattern and swirl of fur, elegance of movement, perfection of form. Delicacy of whisker, brilliance of eye, gentleness of outstretched paw and loving, butting head. Expressiveness of tail. Complexity of ear. A mouth of pink and ivory, curved tongue and shining teeth. A voice of mystery.

APRIL 28

There are
a thousand kinds
of Dog.
There is one Cat.

Kit, Katten, Cat. Charm.
Mischief. Wisdom.

Cats only relish
the highlights of their
day. Food, cuddles,
hunting, washing,
play. And sleep
the rest away.

She has no words,
but by small touchings
and buttings, she shows
her love for you and tries
to distract you
from your sorrow.

APRIL 30

Backs to the wall.
The cat is in galloping mode.

All treasured.
All mourned, however long
or short their existence.
Cats leave their imprint
on the years that can never
be erased.

A dog loves
to be laughed at.
A cat takes a long while
to forgive you.

SEPTEMBER 3

We hold every cat
that we have ever had safe
in our hearts forever.

Cat.
Remember me.
Come home.

We play together.
Doze away the summer
afternoons together.
Rest in a shared
contentment.
You are part of our family
– what would we do
without you?

A kitten believes all things
are permissible
so long as they are fun.

SEPTEMBER 1

IT IS GOOD
TO KEEP A CAT.
THEY FORCE US
TO REALIZE
WE ARE NOT
THE ONLY REALITY.

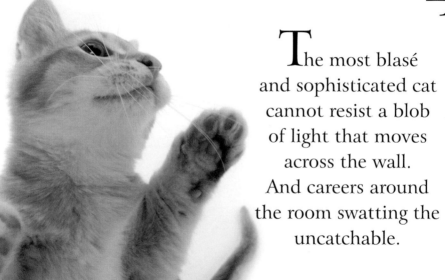

MAY 4

The most blasé
and sophisticated cat
cannot resist a blob
of light that moves
across the wall.
And careers around
the room swatting the
uncatchable.

The gentle touch of
an outstretched paw.
The butt of a head.
…the trust and
affection of a little cat.

Cats, you must realize, have quietly taken over the world.

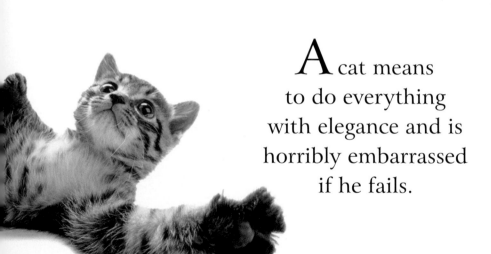

AUGUST 30

A cat means
to do everything
with elegance and is
horribly embarrassed
if he fails.

Cats are masters
of the art
of infiltration.

No cat is as virtuous
as he looks.

"As helpless
as a kitten"
is a nonsense.
Kittens cope.

AUGUST 28

I call into the night.
He sits in shadow
and listens.
Appreciating my
anxiety.
Biding his time.

To a dog, dinner is dinner. To a cat it is a source of amusement and invention.

AUGUST 27

Stop scratching
your cat for one moment
and a single paw reaches
out and reminds you
to resume.

A dog forgives
his tormentors.
A cat never quite
forgets.

AUGUST 26

Kittens take us in hand very soon in their lives. They summon us to play. They sulk if put down from our knees. They hog the bed.

A cat can learn
a multitude of skills
if it suits him.

A kitten brings
a joy out of
all proportion
to its size.

"Ah," say the dog owners
"He's nearly human".
Cat owners would not dare.

The cat stands
in the doorway.
"Come. At once.
I need the tap
turned on."

A very small cat
can dominate
a household.

AUGUST 23

You may love me,
says cat.
On my terms.

A dog performs to delight
his owner,
a cat to delight himself.

AUGUST 22

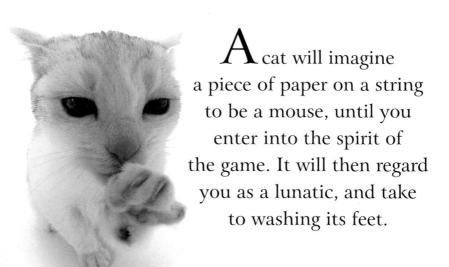

A cat will imagine
a piece of paper on a string
to be a mouse, until you
enter into the spirit of
the game. It will then regard
you as a lunatic, and take
to washing its feet.

Try me in a harness?
Don't be ridiculous.

A dog goes on loving, however he is treated. A cat walks out and finds another home.

A cat can out-think
and outmanoeuvre
any human being.

A dog will pursue
a thrown ball,
and bring it back.
A cat will sit under
a chair, swipe the ball
– and let the thrower
retrieve it.

A reformed street cat
can be the sweetest
natured of them all.

How comforting
the gentle snoring
of a little cat.

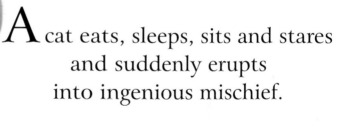

A cat eats, sleeps, sits and stares
and suddenly erupts
into ingenious mischief.

AUGUST 18

No need to watch
oneself, or act a part.
One's cat knows one
is fairly stupid –
but doesn't mind.

Unfortunately, cats have never faced the fact that humans have no fur or that subsequently play fights draw blood. And indignation.

A cat will show
its outer beauty
to the world and
perhaps hint at its
affectionate heart.
All else is hidden, kept
for the one it loves.

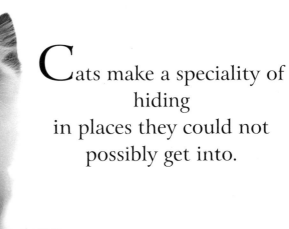

Cats make a speciality of
hiding
in places they could not
possibly get into.

Cats bring a little magic to the dullest life. A little mystery. The scent of wild green places, of darkness and adventure.

To some blind souls
all cats are much alike.
To a cat lover every cat
from the beginning
of time has been
utterly and
amazingly unique.

A CAT GETS WHAT
HE WANTS.

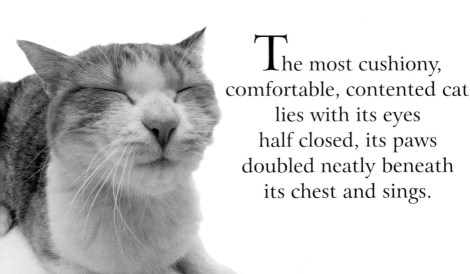

MAY 21

The most cushiony,
comfortable, contented cat
lies with its eyes
half closed, its paws
doubled neatly beneath
its chest and sings.

AUGUST 14

A cat needs
to touch you now
and then
for reassurance.

It doesn't matter
if you are six feet four
and broad of shoulder,
if a kitten is looking
for a mother-figure
you're it.

"Can't you see it?
Can't you smell it?
Can't you hear it?"
the little cat asks.
And regretfully
we shake our heads.

MAY 23

Human beings are
drawn to cats because
they are all we are not
– self-contained,
elegant in
everything
they do, relaxed,
assured.

Mankind takes itself
too seriously.
Kittens are a most
effective cure.

Cats are mysterious, elegant, beautiful. Cats are ridiculous, unpredictable ...and deeply disobedient. Love as they choose to love. Cats are who they decide to be.

AUGUST **11**

How airily our cats
summon and dismiss us.
And we obey.

Perfectly sensible people
apologise to cats.

AUGUST 10

There is nothing
so downputting as an
exasperated kitten who
has failed to explain
something to you,
despite putting it in
words of one syllable.

An ecstatic cat,
welcoming you home,
can purr so loudly
it makes you laugh out
loud with joy.

There is nothing so asleep as a kitten.

Dear cat,
exasperating cat,
we love you.
We turn to you
in sadness,
in loneliness,
in sickness. Dear cat.
Dear comfort.
Dear friend.

There are quiet, shy, gentle kittens, and comic, bold as brass kittens. And all beautiful. And all needing a human being who will think them the very best kitten in the universe.

Cats know, quietly
and with complete
conviction,
that they are
the superior species.

Any cat knows
the precise cost of every
form of cat food
and chooses, unfailingly,
the most expensive.

Do not confuse
the implements in
your cat's feet
with simple claws.
They are excavators,
stilettos, slings, lancets,
rippers of curtains,
engravers of furniture.

W̲ho needs TV
when there's
a kitten around?

A cat asleep
in the garden
is wrapped
around in scent
and birdsong.

If a cat is Disgusted,
it's no good tempting it
with a twitching string.
You are inviting a look
of withering disdain
that would sit
well on a duchess.

Cat has always
known his lineage
was more distinguished
than any Pharoah.
And has lived his
life accordingly.

Cats have never
yet grasped the concept
of No.

A cat could talk
if he wanted to.
But he doesn't.

AUGUST 3

Many an ancient tomcat has a kitten's heart.

Cat owners spend
most of their days
trying to out-think
their cats.

The agitated meow, the frantic meow is "You've been out for hours and, look, my bowl is empty!"

How small
a creature
to hold
one's heart.

AUGUST 1

A pup likes to be laughed at. The smallest kitten is mortally offended.

The beauties
of an ordinary cat
can fill a drowsy
afternoon with wonder.
No need for long
safaris – the marvel
purrs upon your lap.

Old ladies, after a lifetime of dealing with people, find the company of cats a great relief. Cats being companionable and kind, courteous in their dictatorial demands, delicate in their greed, clean, beautiful and elegant… And vulnerable as we all are.

To possess a cat
is to be a part
of a worldwide
company
of devoted slaves.

A cat loves to hear
you calling its name.
It will listen contentedly
for an hour at a stretch.
Of course, it won't
respond – only listen.

Cats wrap themselves in summer as in a coverlet.

A cat is never bored. At a loose end he will remove all... the keys from their hooks, climb the north face of the bookcase or eat the rubber plant.

Cat owners sometimes
have an ugly suspicion
that the Lord
of the Universe
has whiskers and a long,
ginger tail.

A cat stalks into
the living room.
"Put down everything.
It's time to play".

A cat expects
a chair at
the dinner table.
Especially
if it's formal.

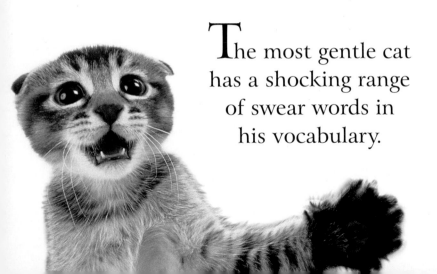

The most gentle cat
has a shocking range
of swear words in
his vocabulary.

A cat never ceases to be astounded by your stupidity. After all, he has explained a dozen times how to open the back door.

Cats arrange
themselves
to present
the best effect.

I don't think the word "relax"
was invented until the discovery of The Cat.

So small a creature
to make so great a difference
to your life.

The loss
of a cat never
quite heals.

Only those who do
not have a cat
say that cats can't talk.

Albert moved in after having explored the possibilities of most other houses in the street. Good garden, a woman who was obviously a kindly, easily-persuaded mug.

Cats bring
the scent of summer
home on their fur.

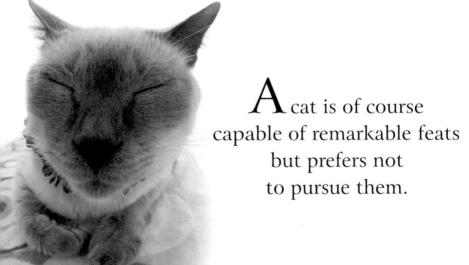

A cat is of course
capable of remarkable feats
but prefers not
to pursue them.

A cat who doesn't
want to, won't.

One small cat
changes coming home
to an empty house
to coming home.

Never give your
friend's cat
the food your cat
won't eat.
Give it a fortnight
and he'll eat
nothing else.

A cat's paw
is built for flicking.
Food pellets.
Water. Clocks. Vases.
The contents of
a larder.

JULY 20

Dogs live with you,
cats board with you.

A cross kitten
comes across the room,
burning with rage
– his fur on end.
At all costs do
not laugh at him.
A kitten has his pride.

E ven the most
sober-minded cat
is capable of a
Funny Half Hour.

You own a dog but you feed a cat.

A cat deflates
the largest ego by merely
narrowing its eyes.

JUNE 18

How good it is
to live with a cat
– for a cat does not
look for perfection,
only food, shelter
a cuddle when he needs
it, and someone adept
at stroking.

The possession
of a cat links
mankind the whole
world over.

A bored cat,
a restless cat.
Or asleep.

A cat loves
to help you tidy
your papers.

All kittens set
out to teach their
humans to adapt
to the needs of a cat.
As a reward,
they grant them
the position
of honorary cat.

JULY 15

In mid chase
she stops. Sits. Washes
her feet. Stares at you
with disapproval.
"For heaven's
sake woman,"
she declares.
"Act your age."

A richly
contented purr
can drown
the radio.

Kittens undermine pomposity.

JUNE 22

A cat is
the bridge that links us
to the wild wood
and the time
beyond time.

Cats give us life.
Sleeping, tuning
their heartbeats to our own,
singing away sorrow,
unravelling the day.

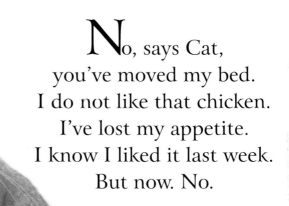

No, says Cat,
you've moved my bed.
I do not like that chicken.
I've lost my appetite.
I know I liked it last week.
But now. No.

JULY **12**

A cat
believes in
privacy.
His.
Not yours.

JUNE 24

After scolding
one's cat one looks
into its face and is seized
by the ugly suspicion
that it understood
every word. And has
filed it for reference.

JULY 11

The shabbiest cat
has the mark
of ancient royalty
about him.

Never let
a cat near a man
with a wig.

A small cat
stretches out its paw
to touch your face
and you are no longer
lost or lonely.

For a kitten
the world is
an enchantment.
A challenge.

You have been calling the cat for twenty minutes. He is sitting three yards from you in the shelter of a bush. Amused.

JUNE 27

At best, one
is one's cat's
companion.
At worst,
its slave.

"Come" says master – and the dog comes. "Go" he says – and the dog goes. Use your entire vocabulary on a cat and he will do exactly as he pleases.

Try to photograph
a cat and it will present
the back of his head.
Until you've used up
the film when he will
immediately perform.

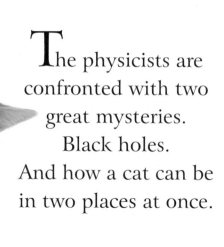

JULY 7

The physicists are confronted with two great mysteries. Black holes. And how a cat can be in two places at once.

A cat has a very
short attention span
unless he's watching
a mouse hole.

Even Fabergé
could never
have fashioned
something as
exquisite in its
detail as a
tiny kitten.

A lost dog is a
pitiable, bewildered
creature. Poor soul.
A lost cat is looking for
an alternative residence.

When the heart
is desolate
a little cat
will warm and
comfort it.

Cat's claws were given to it to hunt, to fight and to climb trees, but centuries have extended its abilities to shin up curtains, open doors, lift lids, and rearrange the ornaments.

He is a kindly cat,
loving beyond reason;
head-butter, nuzzler,
flubsy sprawl of fur,
belly spread, he lies
like an upturned table,
forepaws kneading,
demanding notice
and a rub-a-tum.

Dancers
watch cats,
and sigh
with envy.

A cat may have
a limited vocabulary,
but it can tell you
exactly what it wants,
and will accept no
excuses whatever.